WHERE PEOPLE LIVE

ANGELA ROYSTON

HODDER
Wayland

an imprint of Hodder Children's Books

GEOGRAPHY STARTS HERE!

Where People Live

OTHER TITLES IN THE SERIES
Hills and Mountains · Maps and Symbols
Rivers and Streams · Weather Around You
Your Environment

Produced for Wayland Publishers Limited by
Lionheart Books
10, Chelmsford Square
London NW10 3AR
England

Designer: Ben White

Editor: Lionel Bender

Picture Research: Madeleine Samuel

Electronic make-up: Mike Pilley, Radius

Illustrated by Rudi Visi

First published in Great Britain in 1997
by Wayland (Publishers) Ltd
Reprinted in 2002 by Hodder Wayland,
an imprint of Hodder Children's Books
© Hodder Wayland 1997

British Library Cataloguing in Publication Data
Royston, Angela
Where people live. – (Geography starts here!)
1. Geography – Juvenile literature
I. Title II. Bender, Lionel
910

ISBN 0 7502 4157 8

Printed and bound in Hong Kong

Picture Acknowledgements
Pages 2: James Davis Travel Photography. 5: James Davis Travel Photography.
6-7: Zefa/Stockmarket/D. C. Johnson. 7: Wayland Picture Library. 8: Eye Ubiquitous/Hugh Rooney.
9: James Davis Travel Photography. 10: Zefa Photo Library. 11: Wayland Picture Library.
12: Eye Ubiquitous/L. Fordyce. 13: Zefa Photo Library. 14: Zefa/Orion Press. 15: Eye Ubiquitous/M.
Feeney. 16: Eye Ubiquitous/David Cumming. 17: Aerofilms/Wayland. 18: Wayland Picture Library.
19: Zefa Photo Library. 20: Eye Ubiquitous/Adina Tovy Amsel. 21: James Davis Travel Photography.
22: FLPA/L. Lee Rue. 23: Impact Photos/Christophe Bluntzer. 24: DAS/David Simson. 25: James
Davis Travel Photography. 26: Wayland Picture Library/Chri s Fairclough. 27: Wayland Picture
Library. 28: Zefa Photo Library. 29: James Davis Travel Photography. 31: Wayland Picture Library.

The photo on the previous page shows a view over the city of Rio de Janeiro, Brazil.

CONTENTS

ALL OVER THE WORLD

There are nearly 6 billion people living on the Earth. Each of us needs somewhere to rest and sleep. Some people live in tents, others on boats or in caravans, but most people live in a house or an apartment.

Where do you live? You may live in the countryside or in a town or city. Your nearest neighbour may be next door or far away.

This map shows the world's major cities.

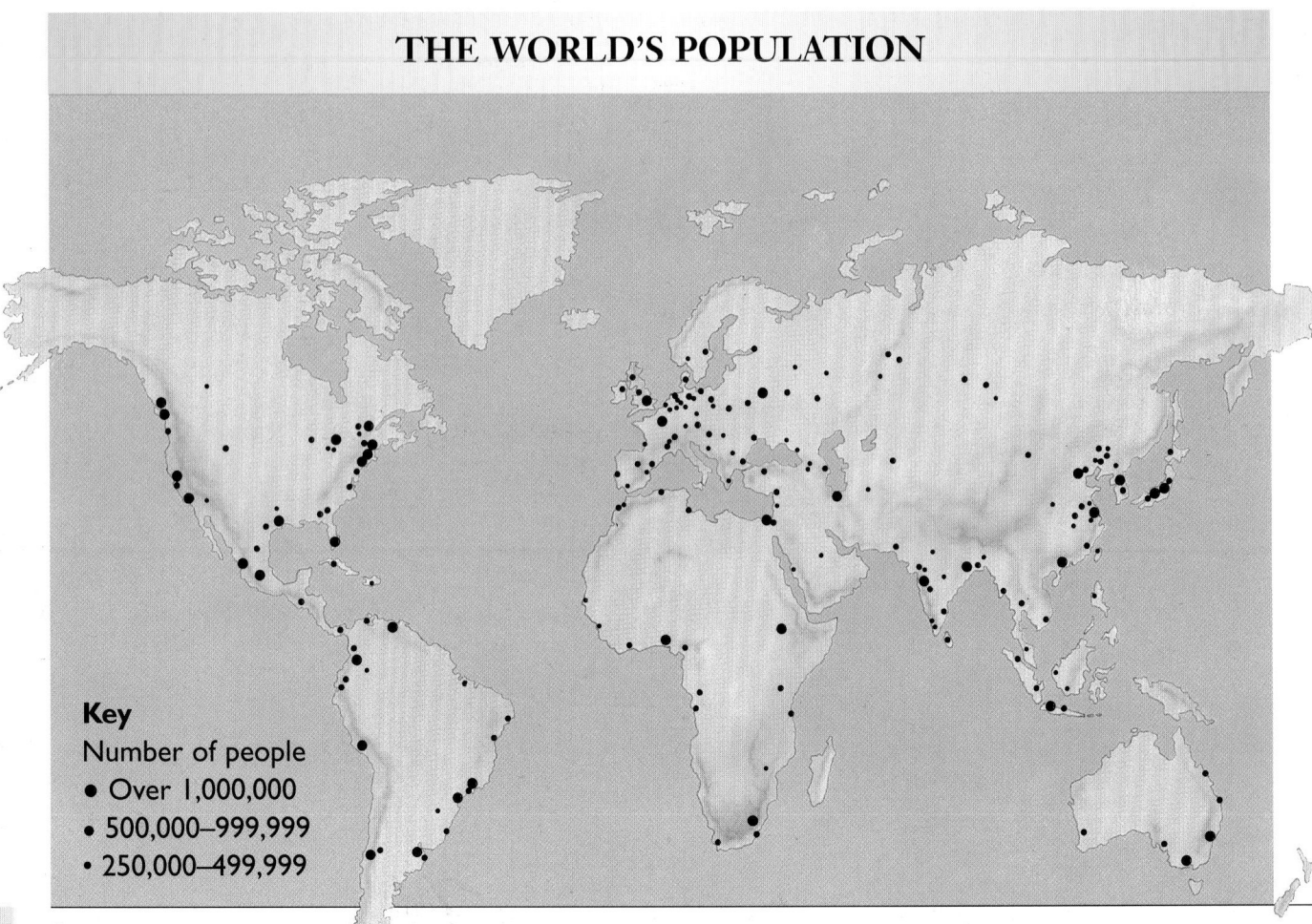

THE WORLD'S POPULATION

Key
Number of people
● Over 1,000,000
● 500,000–999,999
• 250,000–499,999

Houses overlook canals in Venice, Italy. Boats called gondolas ferry people around the city.

SETTLEMENTS

A settlement is a place where people live. There are many different kinds of settlement, from small villages to big cities.

Wherever they live, people need food, water and shelter. They also need fuel for cooking, heat and light.

Large, nineteenth-century houses line streets in San Francisco, USA.

In some places people grow food and collect their own water and firewood. But in many places, people have jobs and buy everything they need from shops and markets.

A postman with his camel delivers mail to a small settlement in Rajasthan, India.

The Ideal Place

In the past, people built settlements where there was plenty of water, food and fuel. They often chose places by the sea or on a river where they could trade with people from other places.

Trade is very important today. Factories are built close to fast roads and ports so that goods can be transported quickly. The factories also provide jobs, attracting many people to move to these areas.

High-rise homes surround the harbour at Monte Carlo, Monaco.

A crowded street market in London, England. Here, people can buy food, clothes and household goods.

FROM VILLAGES TO CITIES

These houses are in the Highland region of Scotland. In much of Scotland there is only a small number of houses in a huge area of countryside.

All around the world, billions of people live in small villages and towns in the countryside.

Villages look different in each region of the world. Builders use local materials – stone, brick, wood or mud – and design the houses to suit the weather conditions of the region.

In small villages most people know each other. They meet in the local shop and their children go to the same school.

Boats carry goods and people to and from this coastal town in Portugal.

Towns

Villages often grow into towns as industry develops or because the weekly markets attract local farmers. Some become holiday centres in the mountains or by the sea.

Some towns grow into cities. People move there looking for work and more houses are built. Gradually, the city spreads and links with surrounding villages. In some cities the poorest people build their own homes in makeshift areas called shanty towns.

The people living in these shelters in Dacca, Bangladesh have just arrived from the countryside.

This hilltop monastery overlooks a small town in Spain. Most of the houses were built around it during the Middle Ages.

Washing hangs out of the windows of this tall apartment building in Singapore.

Cities

Buildings in city centres include offices, large shops and hotels. Skyscrapers fit in as many people as possible by piling lots of floors on top of each other in tall buildings.

Houses and small factories are usually built around the city centre in the suburbs. Some suburbs have their own shops, schools, parks and cinemas.

Skyscraper offices and apartment blocks tower over Tokyo, Japan.

Capital Cities

Each country has a capital, or most important, city. The leader of the country usually lives in the capital and the main government buildings are here too.

Traffic fills the streets in Bangkok, the capital of Thailand.

A capital city has fast roads or railways to link it with the rest of the country. Capital cities also have airports so people can fly to other cities or to other countries.

This aerial view of London, the capital of England shows parkland, houses, factories, docks and the River Thames.

ON THE MOVE

The most convenient way to get from one place to another is by car, but too many cars jam the streets. Every city has several different forms of transport to help people move about more easily.

Many people cycle to and from work in the rush-hour in Beijing, the capital of China.

Which is the fastest means of transport? On a regular long journey, record the time it takes when you travel by car, bus, bicycle and on foot. Which is the fastest way? Traffic jams can often make car journeys by far the slowest.

Buses or trams each carry up to 100 people. Smaller buses and taxis take people short distances. Trains speed people into and out of city centres. Some cities have trains that run under the ground.

This photo of New York City, USA, shows people on the move by car, taxi and bicycle.

These people are having fun roller skating in Central Park, New York City.

OPEN SPACES

Most cities have parks and gardens, where people can get away from the noise of the traffic. Here they run, play football and other sports, or just relax.

There are many ways to enjoy yourself in a city. You can see famous buildings or visit museums, theatres and cinemas. If you want to buy a souvenir, you can choose from many different kinds of shop and stall.

People sit and relax outside cafés along a canal in Amsterdam, the Netherlands.

UNUSUAL HOMES

Some people live far away from anyone else. In Australia and Argentina, cattle ranches and sheep farms are so big, some farmers use small planes to get to the nearest town.

In most countries farms are much smaller. In India and Africa, many people grow just enough food for themselves with a little over to sell at a local market.

This large sheep farm is in New Zealand.

This family has gathered in front of their mud and straw hut in a tiny village in Kenya, Africa.

In the Mountains

High in the mountains the air is thin and cold. Life is very hard there. Yet thousands of people live in mountain villages.

Many mountain people herd animals and work for tourists and climbers. Some of these people have two homes. In spring and summer they move higher up the mountain where their animals can feed on fresh grass.

People board a bus in the Andes mountains in Ecuador, South America.

HIGH LIFE

On the map on page 4, how many cities can you find on mountains (the light-brown areas)? Living on high mountains is very difficult. But land near mountains gets lots of rain and has many rivers. On the map, are there many cities next to mountains?

This hillside chalet is near the Matterhorn mountain in Switzerland.

Hong Kong is overcrowded. There is no room to build new houses. Many people live on boats called junks.

Living Next to Water

People have always liked to live near water. The sea and rivers provided fish. Rivers also gave a good supply of fresh water. It was easier to travel by boat than over the land.

Groups of houses and farmland stretch along the banks of the River Danube in Austria.

Today some of these old settlements have grown into busy ports and towns, but there are still many fishing villages on the coast.

NEW TOWNS AND CITIES

Most cities have grown from villages and towns. But a few cities have been built in the middle of the countryside. New cities are planned to avoid the problems of the old cities, such as overcrowding.

This modern housing area is in Texas, USA. Each house has its own garden and drive. Many houses have swimming pools.

With no traffic, people can shop peacefully and safely in this shopping mall in Atlanta, USA.

New cities have wide streets to take plenty of traffic, and separate paths for people to walk and cycle. Factories are built away from houses. But some people find the new cities are dull places to live.

FACTS AND FIGURES

Largest country
The Russian Federation is the largest country in the world. It is nearly twice as large as Canada, the second largest country. The Russian Federation stretches from Europe to the Pacific and takes eight days to cross by train.

Smallest country
Vatican City is an independent country in the middle of Rome in Italy. It is no bigger than a city park and less than 1,000 people live there.

Highest population
Over 1,200,000,000 people live in China, but India is catching up fast.

Emptiest country
For every person in Western Sahara there is more than a square kilometre of land. This is not surprising because Western Sahara is almost entirely desert.

Most crowded country
Over half a million people live in the tiny country of Macao. It has about 30,000 people in each square kilometre.

Highest city
Lhasa is nearly 4,000 metres above the level of the sea. Lhasa is the main city of Tibet, a mountainous region between China and India. Tibet is sometimes called the 'roof of the world'. It used to be an independent country until it was conquered by China.

Highest capital city
La Paz is in the Andes Mountains in South America. It is the capital of Bolivia and is almost as high as Lhasa.

City with most people
Tokyo, the capital city of Japan, has grown so big it has joined up with nearby Yokohama to form one huge city with about 25 million people. Mexico City and São Paulo are growing fast.

Oldest city
There has been a city at Jericho near Jerusalem in Israel for about 10,000 years.

Coldest town
The coldest town is Oymyakon in Siberia in eastern Russia. The temperature there has fallen to ⁻70° C.

Tallest skyscrapers
Two tower blocks in Kuala Lumpur in Malaysia are 450 metres high – about half as high as a mountain.

Tent homes
Nomads live in deserts. They wander across the land with their animals looking for plants to graze. They carry their tent homes with them.

Floating homes
Some people live in boats rather than houses. In Amsterdam and in London, old barges are homes to many people.

Further Reading

Homes Around the World by Bobbie Calman (Crabtree, 1995).

Houses and Homes by Helen Barden (Wayland, 1995).

Homes in Hot and Cold Places by Simon Crisp (Wayland, 1994)

Planet Earth by Lionel Bender, (Kingfisher, 1993)

Settlements by Fred Martin (Heinemann, 1996).

Towns and Cities by Claire Llewellyn (Heinemann, 1997).

GLOSSARY

Billion A thousand million, that is 1,000,000,000.

Climate The usual kind of weather in a region.

Country An area of land which has its own government. Most people in a country speak the same language.

Fuel Something, such as wood, coal or gas, which is burned to give heat or light.

Government The group of people who run a country. The government decides how much money will be spent on roads, schools, hospitals, the army, and so on.

Local Not far from home.

Polar lands Very cold lands around the North and South Poles where the ground is always covered by ice.

Ranches The name for a farm in the USA.

Restaurant A place where people can buy and eat a meal that has been cooked for them.

Suburbs The outer parts of a town or city, built around its central area.

Trade Buying and selling goods.

Traffic All the vehicles, such as cars, lorries, buses and vans, which move along a road.

A busy street scene in Calcutta, India.

INDEX